written by the light of the Son

F. Toscano II

ISBN-9798580606361

dedication

to the One True God

the Savour of the world

and me

Yeshua

the plea

I'm telling you this because on the other side I do not want you to come up to me and ask, Why did you not tell me? God is real, and just as you and I, he came through the flesh. Jesus was God in the flesh. He could not have done all that he did if he was not. Uncountable miracles he performed, the blind received sight, the deaf received hearing, the lame walked, the lepers were cleansed, demons were cast out, and the dead were brought back to life. He fed multitudes with hardly anything. He walked on water and calmed the storm. The words he spoke are divine. The Holy Bible is completely true and perfect and reality, written by God through the hands of men. I'm telling you this because I want you to be in paradise with us. Heaven is infinite times better than the best things in the flesh, but the other side of Heaven is infinite times worse than the worst things here. We cannot even begin to fathom such things with the limited wisdom possible for us to achieve. If you have doubt, just ask him for faith, and when he reveals himself to you, he will take you deeper into his kingdom. There is no better place on earth, or beyond.

table of contents

before the beginning   9

the beginning   21

the book   31

the king   67

the enemy   133

the end   153

before the beginning
2019

fore the foundation of the world
in the first age what did exist
that which to forever persist
where without time a time unfurled

heaven and earth tightly knitted
and this to forever remain
the earth created not in vain
but formed to be inhabited

to become void and without form
at the birth of the second age
the result of a Fathers rage
in little time his heart to warm

the blind the messenger pities
the truth for those with eyes to see
the flesh a limited journey
between the two eternities

the rotations around the sun
the age of the terra and fount
a number no mere man can count
to when this all might have begun

kolaiah
2013

I can bring dead things back to life
as I was here before the start
I can change minds so vastly rife
and I can harden any heart

I tear the universe apart
I can bring dead things back to life
I created the work of art
I treat everything as my wife

I can release religious strife
but it is free will I impart
I can bring dead things back to life
everything dies when I depart

no chance for my weak counterpart
he leapt upon a righteous knife
all he destroys I can restart
I can bring dead things back to life

quatern 543
2018

I've loved you since the first earth age
the time from all the world hidden
before this flesh would now encage
your true being beneath the skin

eternity if to begin
I've loved you since the first earth age
the second now to find Me in
again once for us to engage

a love before all eyes to wage
a war alone for us to win
I've loved you since the first earth age
where our hearts could never harden

peculiar into each to spin
rarely either of us enrage
uncommon we have in common
I've loved you since the first earth age

rondel 503
2018

the two eternities exist
before the flesh and after lay
behind you for you to assay
before you for you to resist

or accept and ever persist
believe and leave behind dismay
the two eternities exist
before the flesh and after lay

the end of every to do list
a thousand years as of a day
a day you sleep a third away
someday i pray you get the gist
the two eternities exist

quatern 637
2020

of all ages there are but three
the truth of time the wise discern
where future and past selves agree
the second at present sojourn

for first and third our souls to yearn
of all ages there are but three
unknown within our spirit churn
a thirst for home as if at sea

the flame of fleshly hell to flee
a hunger for the hearth to burn
of all ages there are but three
eternity through two to earn

the first in the second unlearn
the third for sometime soon to be
our former glory to return
of all ages there are but three

quatern 137
2012

fore earth was twisted in her path
for once again we will be there
in this flesh ages aftermath
where every single soul stripped bare

and everyday the weather fair
fore earth was twisted in her path
for justice we must now prepare
for rudiments a cleansing bath

and now praise God for all you hath
for soon of nothing He will spare
fore earth was twisted in her path
He promised everyone their share

as if in two the world did tear
the fallout of a Fathers wrath
for once again it is my prayer
fore earth was twisted in her path

quatern 202
2014

before abraham Jesus was
before it all even began
and was Immanuel because
it all was according to plan

and to always be rather than
before abraham Jesus was
the entire universe ran
because of everything He does

a perfect path behind Him was
the wise will join His caravan
before abraham Jesus was
from always to forever span

and now i write for Him not man
rather He writes through me because
anything to be done He can
before abraham Jesus was

quatern 625
2020

all of this now before did choose
ahead of passage through the womb
for the fools to believe but ooze
to have witnessed the ancient boom

worry and doubt over to loom
all of this now before did choose
all of the hate and love to bloom
all of the wars and gold to lose

ever ignited every fuse
of flames to fan within the fume
all of this now before did choose
whether to come out of the brume

the past forgotten to exhume
for all amiss miscues excuse
once more return beyond the tomb
all of this now before did choose

all of this now before did choose
the way for the light to illume
for the wise within to enthuse
for true existence to resume

rondel 522
2018

you must come out from under world
escape the vanity of man
arise to before this began
the age of flesh had yet unfurled

through waves of time whichever purled
where every soul as children ran
you must come out from under world
escape the vanity of man

about this askew axis birled
past pandemonium to pan
cross all kingdoms cleansing flames fan
again earth to as it had skirled
you must come out from under world

quatern 421
2016

where time does not exist
not how in it we versed
of an opposing gist
and empty of an erst

the wicked are accursed
where time does not exist
an unjust man will thirst
and within anguish twist

into transparent mist
the foe from within burst
where time does not exist
and need not be rehearsed

within itself submersed
no longer to persist
for we were all there first
where time does not exist

quatern 669
2020

time for me does not exist
the Author of time my clock
within His precision twist
perfection the world to shock

ever through paradise walk
time for me does not exist
within His safe harbor dock
His refuge ever amidst

everything upon the list
easily off it knock
time for me does not exist
linked within His timeline lock

all deadlines for Him to block
while ever his peace persist
forever with Him to talk
time for me does not exist

quatern 598
2019

before You opened my eyes
through nightmare did i maunder
mystified by the sunrise
unaware of what yonder

the future not to ponder
before You opened my eyes
the truth the world to launder
escape within stolen lies

hidden within my disguise
i was but an absconder
before You opened my eyes
opportunity squander

knew not You a responder
amidst the blinded unwise
through darkness did i wander
before You opened my eyes

the beginning
2019

the beginning no man has seen
even the first as it does seem
the start for any man to deem
with God would have to come between

He who makes His angels spirit
and within earthen vessels breathe
for souls a casting to enwreathe
a cloak for few never to fit

to be tested through the flesh fires
and through the womb be born anew
a God who would Himself do too
what of His children He requires

man upon birth weak and naive
in innocence to come to be
a babe in unknown hands is he
but what he is taught to believe

quatern 524
2018

behold the beauty of autumn
in the wake of crisis of men
to have been brought to the bottom
ripped from hands everything taken

to the little things awaken
behold the beauty of autumn
break from that which has ever been
a glorious future become

of all which cannot change benumb
a present biography pen
behold the beauty of autumn
the nature of youth forsaken

upon solid ground through the fen
out of primordial ooze from
design of a God unshaken
behold the beauty of autumn

rondel 528
2018

the meaning of life salvation
all else you seek a far second
as fleeting as a gust of wind
rise and fall kingdom and nation

irrelevant in life station
for all of this age will rescind
the meaning of life salvation
all else you seek a far second

as far as heavens creation
past clockworks Father to unwind
the reason angels suit mankind
come blind to find true elation
the meaning of life salvation

rapid
2013

has been but a couple of days
from whence our Savior sacrificed
uninevitably enticed
by something of which He would raze

an evil so great to amaze
while the perfect Messiah priced
has been but a couple of days
from whence our Savior sacrificed

Christianity set ablaze
a supreme surrender sufficed
since on the earth in flesh walked Christ
the only One worthy of praise
has been but a couple of days

rondel 469
2017

the calendar His birth upturned
time to end and begin again
His coming droves before to pen
the Word of God within them burned

His deity the masses spurned
though witnessing miracle then
the calendar His birth upturned
time to end and begin again

as all must this age He sojourned
in flesh God to walk among men
unlike what will be as has been
within a virgin womb concerned
the calendar His birth upturned

quatern 327
2015

in the flesh we are but arrayed
imprisoning the truth shackles
a dungeon useless to evade
coupled to the world in rackles

as jesters in scoffing cackles
in the flesh we are but arrayed
upon the spirit in spackles
in illusion essence inlaid

a covering becoming frayed
a clay overlaid in crackles
in the flesh we are but arrayed
soon carried away by jackals

temporary tabernacles
a fleeting shroud away to fade
shedding every body tackles
in the flesh we are but arrayed

rondel 472
2017

it is but an imperfect age
in due the bell upon to chime
defy the laws of man and time
this world of vanity upstage

within you to subdue rampage
enter a serene peace sublime
it is but an imperfect age
in due the bell upon to chime

the truth of mans lies to uncage
from their proverbial to climb
and walk not crawl out of their slime
with the one true God to engage
it is but an imperfect age

rondel 558
2019

a new year of faith to begin
a year past of bondage behind
the bounds wound all around unbind
a freedom unfound to fall in

as skin shed the shackles of sin
the fact of salvation to find
a new year of faith to begin
a year past of bondage behind

defeat the wickedness within
no longer to be deaf and blind
unclutter your eyes and your mind
believe the truth to man hidden
a new year of faith to begin

rondel 531
2018

all flesh it is born in sin
in every body the urge
over and over the verge
tempting is the forbidden

a force never to ridden
part of you never to purge
all flesh it is born in sin
in every body the urge

from the loins our origin
midst thousands of foes we surge
from the womb must we emerge
to this wicked age come in
all flesh it is born in sin

rondel 332
2015

believing in evolution
is he with the mind of an ape
from an evil invention drape
theoretical pollution

an essence in execution
from extinction without escape
believing in evolution
is he with the mind of an ape

distortion of absolution
a mind to deception agape
creation by man to misshape
but a satanic solution
believing in evolution

the book
2019

a time foretold of certain fate
a book trusted by divine men
proven true over and again
the past and future illustrate

the truth proclaimed by men of old
ancient wisdom harmonious
with modern mans chaotic muss
as counsel of ancestors mold

through prophecy with evidence
of what has been after written
so accurate all doubt smitten
given faith in future events

in tales beyond faithless belief
of mans limited mind the law
defy within inspiring awe
to enhearten the deepest grief

quatern 320
2015

the Book from which all books come from
a fantastic tale to enthrall
not but of what great men have done
but that which is still to befall

the handwriting upon the wall
the Book from which all books come from
for the meek victory withal
against great odds to overcome

a year of days is as but one
before you walk you first must crawl
the Book from which all books come from
only for whom they hear the call

a King is born within a stall
the greatest sacrifice a son
for salvation a chance for all
the Book from which all books come from

rondel 643
2020

the profound Word of the Lord
as forever horizon
with the fangs of a lion
as the two edges of sword

forever His bride adored
His most heavenly zion
the faithful Word of the Lord
as surrounding horizon

the foundation now explored
the most Ancient of days from
to His new jerusalem
ever i to walk toward
the perfect Word of the Lord

karkaa
2013

Your Word for all the world in print
the truth for they You will entrust
Your essence is omnipresent
Your Spirit inside souls robust

for men of the earth are but dust
Your Word for all the world in print
the treasure of the earth to rust
while heavens treasure permanent

Your charity omnipotent
never from You to wanderlust
Your Word for all the world in print
submission to it to adjust

Your righteous wrath and anger just
and Your forgiveness omniscient
to evil Your pure counterthrust
Your Word for all the world in print

quatern 549
2018

through hands of men written by God
of that which will be and has been
a truth for lost to find but odd
of miracles to come again

a Word above all words to laud
written by God through hands of men
with a correlation unflawed
for more than forty souls to pen

beyond the bounds of worldly ken
throughout the universe abroad
written by God through hands of men
the origin of man unthawed

either trod through an endless fen
ever about the foes den plod
or stroll throughout heavenly glen
through hands of men written by God

quatern 405
2016

cast forth unto the tempest wave
a great fish prepared to be fed
three days within internal cave
out of the belly of hell pled

the weeds were wrapped about his head
cast forth unto the tempest wave
the depths closed round about with dread
down to the bottom where none brave

of earth her bars no man to save
laid to rest on the ocean bed
cast forth unto the tempest wave
the soul with fainting to be wed

spewed forth of the mariners dead
rescued from the watery grave
no more of the sea to be bled
cast forth unto the tempest wave

rondel 328
song of solomon 8:7
2015

many waters cannot quench love
and neither can the floods drown it
love is stronger than death to wit
for it is a gift from above

look into the eyes of your dove
in an abode but candlelit
many waters cannot quench love
and neither can the floods drown it

for love the man to give all of
the substance of his house for it
is far richer than he befit
all the worlds gold to receive of
many waters cannot quench love

rondel 329
ecclesiastes 5:12-14
2015

whether he have little or much to eat
for so as he came forth so shall he leap
thereof to his hurt his riches to heap
do become naught for his son to entreat

by evil travail those riches do cheat
out of the happiness of life to reap
whether he have little or much to eat
for so as he came forth so shall he leap

sore evil under the sun to defeat
that of a rich man for which he to keep
abundance will not suffer him to sleep
the sleep of a laboring man is sweet
whether he have little or much to eat

rondel 652
genesis 8:22
2020

while to remain the land and sea
until from this earth age release
summer and fall will never cease
winter and spring ever to be

cold and heat from never to flee
day and night ever the Lords fleece
while to remain the land and sea
until from this earth age release

ever to grow the grass and tree
seedtime and harvest in the crease
only under the Son at peace
the climate controlled but by He
while to remain the land and sea

rondel 176
psalms 96 and 97
2014

clouds and darkness are round about
a fire goes before elegance
let the sea roar with fullness rinse
the multitude of isles about

let the field be joyful and tout
the trees of the wood rejoice since
clouds and darkness are round about
a fire goes before elegance

hills melt as wax in his presence
light sown for the righteous to sprout
lightning enlightens with a shout
heaven and earth bow to the Prince
a fire goes before elegance

rondel 642
nahum 1:3-15
2020

beneath His feet the clouds are dust
His way in the whirlwind and storm
your vow and solemn feast perform
pass through you no more the unjust

for He knows them that in Him trust
stronghold in the day of reform
beneath His feet the clouds are dust
His way in the whirlwind and storm

burning fury from the earth crust
the hills and the mountains deform
as all of His enemies swarm
as stubble devoured combust
beneath His feet the clouds are dust

passage
numbers 10:35
2013

rise up Lord for Your day to be
the heathens unbelief shattered
them that hate Thee flee from Thee
let Thine enemies be scattered

let Thine enemies be scattered
them that hate Thee flee from Thee
the heathens unbelief shattered
rise up Lord for Your day to be

rondel 471
revelation 9:14-18
2017

loose the angels four it must be
bound in the great river have been
an hour day month and year when
the angels were to be set free

two hundred million man army
for to slay the third part of men
loose the angels four it must be
bound in the great river have been

with breastplates on horses mighty
with the heads of lions and then
out of their mouths once and again
fire smoke and brimstone all three
loose the angels four it must be

rondel 459
zechariah 9:10-14
2017

I will end the time of trouble
return ye prisoners of hope
horse and chariot cease to lope
the battle bow in hands rubble

wherein no water does bubble
out of the pit earthen walls grope
I will end the time of trouble
return ye prisoners of hope

with whirlwinds yielding but stubble
arrows as lightning down to slope
the trumpet blown no flesh to cope
I will render unto double
I will end the time of trouble

quatern 317
daniel 8:23-25
2015

a king of fierce countenance nigh
shall destroy wonderfully grand
when the transgressors multiply
and are come to the full command

dark sentences shall understand
a king of fierce countenance nigh
mighty but not by his own hand
his power and practice a lie

his policy which he shall by
cause craft to prosper in his hand
a king of fierce countenance nigh
by peace shall destroy many and

against the Prince of princes stand
himself in his heart magnify
he shall be broken without hand
a king of fierce countenance nigh

quatern 131
2012

its all part of the master plan
first the fraud with a show grand
antichrist in the eyes of man
a chosen few to understand

its set in perfect motion and
its all part of the master plan
the future is in every hand
a book that starts when time began

so search as often as you can
and for the perfect truth demand
its all part of the master plan
for those who enter promise land

the few who in this time withstand
in paradise forever span
when Jesus comes the flesh is sand
its all part of the Masters plan

rondel 554
2018

the tainted air they make us breathe
from behind their prisons concrete
their weapon now being discreet
intentions soon they shall unsheathe

the life within the earth unwreathe
despoil the ground beneath your feet
while tainted air they make us breathe
from behind their prisons concrete

Your two edged Word within ensheathe
the world over ever repeat
the Vine enwrapping earth complete
the Heir ever in me enwreathe
for tainted air they make us breathe

rondel 420
2016

there is but one Immanuel
a virgin did conceive anew
a sign from God to have come true
many a prophet to foretell

hereof to come for death to quell
the anointed of God hereto
there is but one Immanuel
a virgin did conceive anew

God in the flesh with man to dwell
to do that which we all must do
of a woman the womb come through
the one true God of israel
there is but one Immanuel

rondel 415
2016

the cup of gethsemane
which Jesus wanted to pass
is for the unholy mass
they with His Word disagree

the cup we are yet to see
the end for many alas
the cup of gethsemane
which Jesus wanted to pass

to pour on the enemy
the one true Gods righteous wrath
with heaven the aftermath
and so done Thy will to be
the cup of gethsemane

rondel 476
2017

a babe in the arms of the Lord
for peace and joy His love assured
nourished as though a baby bird
just as an only child adored

within His safe harbor aboard
flourished within His waters stirred
a babe in the arms of the Lord
for peace and joy His love assured

behind His shield ahead His sword
His armor about me to gird
given wisdom within His Word
salvation the greatest reward
a babe in the arms of the Lord

quatern 582
2019

while all surrounding paradise
to and fro twixt heaven and hell
at present but one to entice
upon the other fate befell

through fruitless gardens carousel
while all surrounding paradise
the valley of death by day dwell
where secrets of soon bliss suffice

a Word limitless and precise
all that was and will be foretell
while all surrounding paradise
a lure upon the heart compel

spirit become while the flesh quell
previously was paid the price
enter before you sigh farewell
while all surrounding paradise

quatern 328
2015

venturing out of the most bold
amidst weakness fell victory
divinity unto behold
another kind of majesty

trust in divine nobility
venturing out of the most bold
that preordained tried to vary
unlike how believed to unfold

and yet so long ago foretold
within shame came a destiny
venturing out of the most bold
out of weeping rained surety

from a rock grew prosperity
that solid easily to mold
to spread this gospel globally
venturing out of the most bold

rondel 626
2020

i see salvation
in the holy book
trickle as a brook
to every nation

solid foundation
heaven and earth shook
i see salvation
in the holy book

the one oblation
the worlds reproach took
to Yeshua look
ever elation
i see Salvation

rondel 380
2016

conduction for the greatest source
of power in the universe
an energy into submerse
to freely submit to this force

the widow of this world divorce
the light in your heart to coerce
conduction for the greatest source
of power in the universe

the bible of this to endorse
vitality in every verse
a new potential to disperse
through your spirit complete the course
conduction for the greatest source

revival
2011

open your eyes your ears your mind
and wipe the dust from your bible
for too long have you been idle
and now you are so far behind

you have no clue what you will find
look and you will see an eyeful
open your eyes your ears your mind
and wipe the dust from your bible

inside the words of all outshined
inside of you a revival
of what to you is most vital
a light so glorious you're blind
open your eyes your ears your mind

rondel 537
2018

the carnal mind cannot fathom
therefore ever to fluctuate
within the wee beyond the great
the universe to an atom

til the bitter end from adam
confusion to perpetuate
the carnal mind cannot fathom
therefore ever to fluctuate

deep as a bottomless chasm
the measure not to calculate
a book ago did illustrate
to unbelievers phantasm
the carnal mind cannot fathom

rondel 598
2019

honor even when dishonored
even when stolen from steal not
murder never do nor do plot
let not your borne witness be blurred

upon loins monogamy gird
never wish a covetous thought
honor even when dishonored
even when stolen from steal not

keep sabbath since it first occurred
the Lords name in vain never brought
graven images ever blot
before no other gods be stirred
honor even when dishonored

rondel 308
2015

as a novel epic beckoned
across this foreign terrain rage
in confusion resistance wage
cast about by a distant wind

an odd script within us summoned
as if performers on a stage
as a novel epic beckoned
across this foreign terrain rage

within this body imprisoned
we are aliens of this age
a liberation from this cage
for soon this flesh it will rescind
as a novel epic beckoned

quatern 652
2020

a page with infinite deckle
essence in boundary unfit
madness becoming but jeckle
to reality tightly knit

overcome the bottomless pit
a page with infinite deckle
upon the wave between the split
the world within wisdom to speckle

undaunted before heckle
ignorance easily outwit
a page with infinite deckle
a spreading out never to quit

fortitude to never forfeit
even unto the last sheckle
never with compromise to sit
a page with infinite deckle

quatern 241
2014

the first Poet and paramount
Your Word in me a melody
without a more truthful account
a miraculous honesty

a fool but to call fantasy
the first Poet and paramount
triumphant but through tragedy
a supernatural surmount

a prophecy on which to count
the coming wrath a canopy
the first Poet and paramount
the strength against the enemy

upon this age the harmony
of the Spirit of life the fount
upon lips divine poetry
the first Poet and paramount

rondel 588
2019

twisting reality until
a fairer fantasy is born
the skin of anyone else worn
but in the end ever me still

upon paper to overspill
oblivion with words adorn
twisting reality until
a fairer fantasy is born

ink upon hides written with quill
from pages of long ago torn
to come to be every oath sworn
for the one true Word to fulfill
twisting reality until

rondel 534
2018

the book in my hands is my sword
the words within my power drawn
the source of my celestial brawn
the Spirit through my spirit poured

filled with divine strength of the Lord
all else around me seems so wan
the book in my hands is my sword
the words within my power drawn

i alter not what i move toward
this wicked ages final dawn
though the enemy fire upon
i hold the eternal reward
the book in my hands is my sword

rondel 663
2020

sear Your seal in my forehead
and write Your truth with my hand
Your Word across pages fanned
by Your Holy Spirit led

only feed me with Your bread
solely but to bear Your brand
sear Your seal in my forehead
and write Your truth with my hand

from my soapbox all You said
upon Your foundation stand
the Rock over worldly sand
in me Your Son in my stead
sear Your seal in my forehead

quatern 614
2020

but within my ear Your whisper
for all knowledge to come from thence
to intelligence the sister
Your wisdom living opulence

of all i hear the only sense
but within my ear Your whisper
the truth which Your Word documents
within my eyes the true glister

as lies try to turn me twister
Your candor brings me congruence
but within my ear Your whisper
while all others leading the dense

from babel burn of foolish gents
Your soothing balm upon blister
remove the evil influence
but within my ear Your whisper

quatern 662
2020

glittering gold God rains on me
His Word ever within my ear
as morning dew His peace gives He
and joy rising of dayspring cheer

His love for me come to endear
glittering gold God rains on me
the meaning of His grace comes clear
unveiling generous mercy

unearned forgiveness setting free
discernment through my passage steer
glittering gold God rains on me
His truth upon my being sear

into a touch of wisdom peer
a world of salvation to be
His Word ever within my ear
glittering gold God rains on me

rondel 664
2020

Yeshua saturate my soul
fill my mind with Your Word only
Wonderful for the world to see
Counsellor for Your divine goal

the mighty God in all control
the everlasting Father be
Yeshua saturate my soul
fill my mind with Your Word only

the Lord our Righteousness in whole
the Root the Branch of life the Tree
the Prince of Peace Your kingdom free
upon my heart Your Word inscroll
Yeshua saturate my soul

the King
2019

He comes on bended knee before
all which His scepter is beneath
His power and Spirit bequeath
to whom behind Him go to war

an uncommon King dreams of peace
ever beset by battle drums
His realm compassed by foes kingdoms
the death about His dream to cease

a King from the beginning wise
renown throughout His reign worldwide
beyond the end of time abide
His allure as every sunrise

from beneath a crown of glory
His strange work His strange act toward
His countrymen in one accord
through night and day to keep them free
take hold of the strength of your Lord
for sore and great and strong His sword
to slay the dragon in the sea

King
2013

glorify and cherish the King
gratitude to the Redeemer
acclaim to the Advocate bring
esteem to the Mediator

homage to the Deliverer
glorify and cherish the King
obedience to the Teacher
the Shepherd appreciating

praises to the Messiah sing
thanksgiving unto the Savior
glorify and cherish the King
willing service to the Master

worship bestow the Creator
the Lord our God idolizing
honor given to the Father
glorify and cherish the King

rondel 235
2014

the reigning King of every age
the Ruler of the universe
for all the wickedness a curse
but for the righteous to uncage

bringing reward for which we wage
upon us for better or worse
the reigning King of every age
the Ruler of the universe

a fair and justified rampage
warned about in many a verse
in which it is we must submerse
if it is that we are to gauge
the reigning King of every age

rondel 201
2014

a goodly price which He was priced
thirty pieces of silver cast
unto the potter strewn aghast
on the floor of the house of Christ

the most iniquitous of heist
sense of the consequences vast
a goodly price which He was priced
thirty pieces of silver cast

for the Kings betrayal sufficed
subsequently but to contrast
the true purpose going unasked
for all of the world sacrificed
a goodly price which He was priced

rondel 383
2016

to the smiters His back He gave
His cheeks to who pulled off the hair
He hid not His face from shames stare
and spitting from they evil crave

falsely accused by rant and rave
not a word of His split the air
to the smiters His back He gave
His cheeks to who pulled off the hair

under a crown of pain to brave
nailed to a tree for all sin fared
His form and visage so impaired
more than all the men he forgave
to the smiters His back He gave

rondel 445
2017

so perfectly
You wore Your skin
from death to win
the victory

setting us free
life to begin
so perfectly
You wore Your skin

You died for me
You bore the sin
i linger in
You lived for me
so perfectly

quatern 635
2020

what was witnessed upon the cross
to the slaughter the Lamb to bring
for His vesture lots they did toss
in four His garments their parting

His hands and feet for their piercing
upon the cross what was witnessed
with the transgressors numbering
all His bones did out of joint twist

more than any man to exist
His visage marred beyond anything
upon the cross what was witnessed
prophecy of old fulfilling

His tongue unto His jaws did cling
within His mouth was found no dross
He was as water outpouring
what was witnessed upon the cross

kaleidoscope
2013

a Man of endless miracle
from His example to be hewn
and to redemption feel Him pull
for whom nobody is immune

everyday with Jesus commune
a Man of endless miracle
with glory let your life be strewn
all of your wounds are healable

and endless promise sealable
inside of His love to cocoon
a Man of endless miracle
the melody of life attune

evil in the world a monsoon
the world it appears to be full
be not of that which He will prune
the Man of endless miracle

rondel 302
2015

as the wind and water obey
the power of life in His hand
sight around blind eyes to band
the might to move mountains away

a pillar of cloud by day
of fire by night a pillar grand
as the wind and water obey
the power of life in His hand

with His strength keep the foe at bay
and through Him the demons command
that not of this world understand
as talking with your best friend pray
as the wind and water obey

kadmiel
2013

Father i so love Your justice
Your ruling is righteous and fair
obvious for all who trust this
a punishment for some to bear

a divine decree to declare
Father i so love Your justice
a perfect verdict everywhere
for some the sentence perfect bliss

the summon of the world to hiss
it is but evil to ensnare
Father i so love Your justice
and for Your return i prepare

the penalty be quite aware
a shame so many will just miss
for the wickeds greatest nightmare
Father i so love Your justice

rondel 550
2018

justice exacted of the Lord
the perfect verdict not blurry
still am i while heathen scurry
deliberate amidst the horde

my enemies have i ignored
unharmed i transcend through fury
justice exacted of the Lord
the perfect verdict not blurry

that not of here revere the sword
and regard not fear and worry
even in death comes victory
for forgiveness have i implored
justice exacted of the Lord

rondel 614
2020

the truth graven upon His palm
a strong hand and an outstretched arm
raining down but the heathen harm
upon elect a healing balm

to disable mans every bomb
and detonate the last alarm
the truth graven upon His palm
a strong hand and an outstretched arm

within complete control to calm
without invitation or smarm
restlessness of the world disarm
upon the end to end all qualm
the truth graven upon His palm

quatern378
2016

Lord both of the living and dead
the universe is Your kingdom
with no deity in Your stead
the earth remains under Your thumb

in every heart to once but hum
Lord both of the living and dead
i wait for You for but a crumb
for my whole lifetime to be fed

without idea where You head
and no notion where You are from
Lord both of the living and dead
mans most mystical conundrum

Your promise for few to fathom
only upon wickedness tread
so the curse causeless shall not come
Lord both of the living and dead

quatern 636
2020

who is the most mysterious
mystique within spirits gyre
to fathom what but weary us
quiescence never acquire

mystify deepest desire
who is the most mysterious
past universal entire
abasing the imperious

whirling the proud delirious
quandary about their ire
who is the most mysterious
setting unquenchable fire

secrets unknowable dire
a wonder upon serious
to paradise His bride squire
who is the most mysterious

rondel 335
2015

who is able to search a heart
to behold deep within the soul
for every existence to dole
for every destiny to chart

for everything designed as art
upon a signature inscroll
who is adept to shape a heart
to behold deep within the soul

to overcome every rampart
to save from the flames of sheol
of all entitled to extol
an endless kingdom to impart
who alone can sire a heart

preoccupied
2013

so far beyond this earthly orb
to You bind me with one accord
my one desire to absorb
with Your Spirit baptize me Lord

to You bind me with one accord
inside my soul to deeply bore
with Your Spirit baptize me Lord
Your truth to retain evermore

inside my soul to deeply bore
my one desire to absorb
Your truth to retain evermore
so far beyond this earthly orb

quatern 595
2019

Your mind is the universe
which You hold within Your hand
true wisdom You to disperse
all dimensions to command

eternity to expand
Your mind is the universe
unable to understand
doubt in faithless to coerce

thus the arrogant accurse
upon unknown planets strand
Your mind is the universe
far beyond just sea and land

while we only grains of sand
within mystery immerse
useless to fathom how grand
Your mind is the universe

quatern 170
2014

with Godspeed upon your journey
the way before you to extend
not the expanse but what you see
the truth bestowed to you to lend

existence a garden to tend
with Godspeed upon your journey
the blessings of life a Godsend
the Author of time setting free

a passage spent on bended knee
between good and evil to rend
with Godspeed upon your journey
to days choose to rightfully spend

a surrounding wall to defend
the quest just a battle to be
a majesty never to bend
with Godspeed upon your journey

rondel 583
2019

in Gods garden glean
where blessings come from
into His kingdom
headlong to careen

somewhere in between
truth and conundrum
where blessings come from
in Gods garden glean

to the world unseen
unfit to fathom
paradise to come
with angels convene
in Gods garden glean

kudzu
2013

the Vine to spread across the land
the Way i wish for You to show
the Truth i wish to understand
the Life alone i wish to know

the Root from which i wish to grow
the Vine to spread across the land
the Light i wish to see the glow
the Word of all the words most grand

the Hope which i could not have planned
the Peace to me You do bestow
the Vine to spread across the land
the Love inside of me You sow

the Friend from which all blessings flow
the Rock on which i wish to stand
the Door through which i wish to go
the Vine to spread across the land

rondel 215
2014

Your patience is eternity
Your love is unfathomable
Your peace is unmeasurable
Your mercy without boundary

Your joy without extremity
Your glory is unstoppable
Your patience is eternity
Your love is unfathomable

Your justice without mystery
Your means are unattainable
Your Word is undefinable
salvation is my victory
Your patience is eternity

rondel 168
2013

my God i vow
my Lord and more
with You i roar
You show me how

to You i bow
with You i soar
my God i vow
my Lord and more

perfection now
salvation for
me evermore
forever Thou
my God i vow

quatern 542
2018

i give it to You
please take it from me
from all this ado
i wish to be free

all i cannot flee
i give it to You
please take it from me
help me be anew

everything askew
no longer to see
i give it to You
please take it from me

all that which to be
all i have gone through
please take it from me
i give it to You

rondelet 173
2020

You Are
my God professed
You Are
my God by far
Your Name be blessed
my Work my Rest
You Are
You Are
my God expressed
You Are
the Door ajar
the Way accessed
my Peace my Quest
You Are

rondel 417
2016

the heir of the air
to reign over rain
in the wain not wane
the fare to find fair

the ware not to wear
the vein not in vain
the heir of the air
to reign over rain

a bare soul to bear
never to fain feign
in plain words to plane
to tear apart tare
the heir of the air

quatern 332
2015

once upon a Kings crusade
heroes armed with but a Word
of nothing to be afraid
from no clash to be deterred

for within victory stirred
once upon a Kings crusade
their armor a Spirit gird
in a glowing Light arrayed

with a lore never to fade
honor in each hero heard
once upon a Kings crusade
evermore every incurred

the foe a dragon inferred
from its underlings inveighed
the conquest of man absurd
once upon a Kings crusade

rondel 468
2017

white knights we fight the red dragon
when darkness shrouds the world in full
our quest is but to quash evil
til from all hearts we vanquish sin

the wickedness which dwells within
out of every being to pull
white knights we fight the red dragon
when darkness shrouds the world in full

in modern times a paladin
of myth refute goddess and bull
in truth it is but the devil
with God the victory to win
white knights we fight the red dragon

quatern 498
2017

in a fine fashion from us we
shall announce the King to enthrone
brandish commandments all to see
declare for what we should atone

gush forth of a wind calmly blown
in a fine fashion from us we
exude a peace to here unknown
mirror the truth to set men free

flash the way to eternity
reflect the light brilliantly shown
in a fine fashion from us we
echo the Word not of our own

display beauty from within grown
exhibit a life graciously
unveil a soul never alone
in a fine fashion from us we

quatern 267
2015

our Father so divine
Your hallowed Name we praise
from heaven where You shine
Your kingdoms golden rays

upon Your will we gaze
our Father so divine
as upon earthly days
in heaven to align

upon Your blessings dine
forgiveness to amaze
our Father so divine
lead through the coming haze

strengthen me in Your ways
and protect me from mine
deliver me from craze
my Father so divine

rondel 539
2018

my King i can hide nothing from
ashamed i bow before Your throne
my service here for You alone
but then i beat a selfish drum

to Your will i wish to succumb
yet give in ever to my own
my King i can hide nothing from
ashamed i bow before Your throne

a better man i have become
for much i still have to atone
Your patience and forgiveness known
my spirit within Yours aplomb
my King i can hide nothing from

rondel 565
2019

the world about me frozen while
i bask in Your glorious light
rudiments ready to ignite
as Your blessings upon me pile

the seas rage surrounding my isle
to a paradise You invite
the world about me frozen while
i bask in Your glorious light

while the wiles of the world beguile
evil upon the earth a blight
uncomplicate Your childs plight
and mitigate my every trial
the world about me frozen while

kiln
2013

engrave Your Word inside my mind
and fill my soul with Your Spirit
truly my life You have aligned
and to You i volunteer it

Your everything i revere it
engrave Your Word inside my mind
my blueprint You engineered it
the universe Your mastermind

Your Name is known to all mankind
and Your voice i long to hear it
engrave Your Word inside my mind
and my future commandeer it

my past i ask and You clear it
and the chains of sin You unbind
through Your love my love endear it
engrave Your Word inside my mind

rondel 612
2020

i see Him come as a Lion
as He was seen come as a Lamb
forever the great King I AM
hailing past even orion

ever surrounding Him zion
heaven His horizon to pan
i see Him come as a Lion
as He was seen come as a Lamb

power of infinite ion
to deliver the sea or damn
the only salvation for man
of entirety the scion
i see Him come as a Lion

quatern 640
2020

than man Gods method far higher
ever unburden of toil
even the old man not tire
nothing to wither or spoil

character never to soil
than man Gods nature far higher
from fear no longer recoil
a new bravery inspire

from worldly belief to gyre
over medicine the oil
than man Gods essence far higher
to miracle remain loyal

a heavenly kingdom royal
the far most sacred of sire
all enemy before foil
than man Gods order far higher

rondel 441
2017

blessings come to a patient man
as life giving rains from above
the faithfulness and peace of dove
across an existence to span

a destiny for none to plan
to tarry for the perfect love
blessings come to a patient man
as life giving rains from above

in rushing waters overrun
into a hastened state to shove
the hurried man running out of
luck coming up short rather than
blessings come to a patient man

sounds of praise
from clouds of grey
2019

under His reign to find refuge
while reward brings about rebirth
the flesh as the grass of the earth
a flourishing within deluge

the life within a flowers love
a husbands endless avowal
fallen tears as sorrowful fowl
the river rapid runs above

the color grey a color grand
in sight to wish not disappear
the sound a symphony in ear
a melody of peace in hand

a sparkle all about to gird
the glitter twinkle in an eye
a pleasure grand no gold to buy
the refreshing a soul in stirred

a blossoming blooming forth from
the rock solid and steadfast stand
exhibiting abundance grand
a beauty never to succumb

to feel it bead upon the face
and all over the body vein
a masterpiece not to remain
in crystal stream art abstract trace

the curtain drawn on torrid blight
the pearl upon the dust ballet
cooling throughout the heat of day
the warmth within the cold of night

in blankets covering careless
spontaneous and slapdash wave
the only lye in worth to lave
the truth of purities bareness

the common link of life the chain
nourishing skies through to the root
fills the face of the world with fruit
a vineyard of grapes blood to stain

blessing upon the humble one
for he on unsure ground a curse
midst oceans of distrust submerse
in blind eyes blotting out the sun

quatern 275
2015

allow the one God carry you
from the womb til the flesh no more
to an unknown love marry you
throughout your spirit to explore

all your days bear your idols or
allow the one God carry you
from whom all charity does pour
to become of the chary few

troubled times aid to tarry through
across this wicked age to soar
allow the one God carry you
to disencumber daily chore

to end inside of you the war
harbor from what would harry you
from crushing waves to come ashore
allow the one God carry you

quatern 353
2016

if within His hands worry not
everything He will shoulder through
with favor your life will be fraught
bestowed upon blessing bestrew

cradle your head the pillow to
worry not if within His hands
to suffer through so much ado
forbearing instigating strands

upheld through your before expands
carried along the way anew
worry not if within His hands
grasp but which understand a few

He formed the universe and you
everything it is He has wrought
by the dust made by fire made true
if within His hands worry not

quatern 211
2014

with the love of God inside him
with joy a man will have life fraught
harvest spilling over the brim
all the blessing repentance brought

to be amidst his presence sought
with the light of God inside him
inside paradise to be caught
in an ocean of bliss to swim

with righteousness not but a whim
the rivals arrows come to naught
with the strength of God inside him
it is a righteous battle fought

doing what most would not have thought
against the world out on a limb
a man who does not need a lot
with the might of God inside him

raffish
2011

with faith defy the laws of man
anythings yours if you believe
the meaning for you to conceive
do whatever you think you can

follow along the perfect plan
forever for you to achieve
with love defy the laws of man
anythings yours if you believe

fight the good fight your whole life span
for transgression there is reprieve
just make it right before you leave
its been this way since time began
with God defy the laws of man

rondel 562
2019

for life endeavor
with faith flesh defy
to your desire die
from yourself sever

wiser than clever
upon truth rely
for life endeavor
with faith flesh defy

fear and doubt never
look death in the eye
his power deny
and live forever
for life endeavor

rondel 538
2018

to something positive be bound
be true but to the righteous cause
your faithfulness devoid of flaws
to whom your vow was wound around

where guile and lie cannot be found
your word in need not of applause
to something positive be bound
be true but to the righteous cause

upon the promise land aground
the bitter cold about you thaws
as ages end it closely draws
your treasure in heaven compound
to something positive be bound

rather
2011

wealth is something rather than gold
and happiness is a warm soul
graciousness should be ever goal
love and truth never to withhold

nothing new forever foretold
what is its worth when the bells toll
wealth is something rather than gold
and happiness is a warm soul

see the world behind a blindfold
always to fall to fill the hole
only Yeshua can console
the meaning and message age old
wealth is something rather than gold

rondel 635
2020

rejoice in others good fortune
cherish when their flourishings thrive
oblige their blossom to revive
only upon your own boughs prune

never to rain upon their june
ever bring their garden alive
rejoice in others good fortune
cherish when their flourishings thrive

eclipse not their sun with your moon
the earth beneath their feet not rive
one in an infinity strive
to be with the perfect attune
rejoice in others good fortune

raindrop
2013

just a small piece of Your power
and of Your love just a raindrop
feeding forever my whole crop
allowing my soul to flower

someday on the whole world shower
eternity never to stop
just a small piece of Your power
and of Your love just a raindrop

all from You never to sour
Your essence here for me to sop
from below raise me to the top
so never again to cower
just a small piece of Your power

quatern 96
2012

for all that You surround me with
i thank You from my heart today
its everyday my heart You lift
i bow to You and walk Your way

for anything i would not stray
for all that You surround me with
my world with righteousness array
ever showing You are no myth

before my soul it was adrift
You brought me back into Your bay
for all that You surround me with
i bow to You and to You pray

You turn to blue my days of grey
You fill my life with every gift
never be able to repay
for all that You surround me with

quatern 78
2011

a glow that will never go out
brightening every tomorrow
a gift for some to figure out
those for which will come to borrow

for those who see ending sorrow
a glow that will never go out
lighting the right way to follow
a guide for some to end all doubt

a goal for some to come about
filling holes no longer hollow
a glow that will never go out
of You it will always be so

on high outshine darkness below
Your love as rain ending the drought
so blessed am i that You bestow
a glow that will never go out

quatern 98
2012

they wish to extinguish my light
my bright glow they try to eclipse
the side they hide that i excite
instead in awe the chance it slips

together blow with lying lips
they wish to extinguish my light
their water all over me drips
raining upon all i ignite

with mounds of sand and out of spite
the hourglass on every flips
they wish to extinguish my light
until every right from me strips

and when you see inside it grips
only one thing could be so bright
the Holy Spirit from me rips
they wish to extinguish my light

quatern 605
2020

a brilliance the world to alight
a difficult poem to pen
a poet alone but polite
a wonder if ever has been

with glimmers faith glitters the den
with brilliance the world to alight
highlands hem in within the glen
with mountains about to ignite

through blessings due to the birthright
passage on dry land through the fen
through brilliance the world to alight
through that never to be again

the unburden to be but when
the end of all which is finite
the mystery all men then ken
the brilliance the world to alight

quatern 644
2020

the poet awry without God
asunder he alone to fade
astray his way his trod façade
amazing for amiss to trade

contrary to the true crusade
the poet averse without God
his will unwilling and afraid
opposed being apart and odd

by perfection of his peers awed
and wonderstruck with words collide
the poet agape without God
astonished his mouth open wide

ever in oceans to abide
wandering waters to maraud
at the mercy of wind and tide
the poet adrift without God

rondel 619
2020

the God of israel and i
together wrote some great poems
His conduit to me He comes
as lightning strikes across the sky

His words through me electrify
before His will my soul succumbs
the God of israel and i
in concert write some great poems

my words for He to beautify
a melody of harp string strums
harmony of heavenly hums
together in accord we tie
the God of israel and i

rondel 504
2018

i live in the hand of the Lord
between His fingers as a quill
upon His words i wait until
for through me his report record

within His plan in one accord
His will before mine to fulfill
i live in the hand of the Lord
between His fingers as a quill

to be His lantern or His sword
for Him to use me as He will
all i to do is lay here still
a treasure in His palm adored
i live in the hand of the Lord

rondel 637
2020

mostly it for You and me
falling from You as the dew
words of happiness anew
with You to ever agree

even if it seen by few
those but close to us to see
mostly it for You and me
falling from You as the dew

within me a silent plea
written for You to bring true
one to be seen but by two
til too looks upon it three
mostly it for You and me

rondel 517
2018

You fill me with Your poetry
not of this world words with Your grace
a rest they without You do chase
a peace for them never to be

within Your perfect harmony
only from Your loving embrace
You fill me with Your poetry
not of this world words with Your grace

my stranded soul You set asea
a passage never to retrace
a passion You show through my face
even unbelievers agree
You fill me with Your poetry

quatern 450
2017

i write which cannot be of me
wonder within am i a fraud
and does the world with me agree
or is this way of thinking flawed

something unknown my prattles prod
i write which cannot be of me
past someone elses conscience plod
to pen of someone elses plea

within my mind i cannot flee
whether at home or far abroad
i write which cannot be of me
for brilliance cannot be of odd

genius for all and i to laud
the truth to set every man free
as though i hear the words of God
i write which cannot be of me

receptacle
2013

i am not so much a writer
as i am the Fathers vessel
in His gracious love to nestle
helping me see His words brighter

making all my burdens lighter
being my proverbial bull
i am not so much a writer
as i am the Fathers vessel

pulling all my writing tighter
on my creative nature pull
within His truth my belief full
for His Word to be a fighter
i am not so much a writer

quatern 628
2020

i His muse to use as He will
the Lord is my song and lyric
His words breathe life into my quill
His voice eternal to my quick

His psalm for me to ever pick
i His muse to use as He will
His ballad am i but one brick
His ever poem to fulfill

His rhythm over me to spill
His rhyme within my veins runs thick
i His muse to use as He will
His hymn upon my heart to stick

His tongue ever upon my wick
His Spirit for i wait until
the Lord is my song and lyric
i His muse to use as He will

rondel 650
2020

only your Word true poetry
for the fool never to fathom
deserted isles his thoughts have swum
while his logic ever asea

for the wise to ever agree
with equation to come to some
only your Word true poetry
for the fool never to fathom

ever alive to grow in me
water the seed i grow up from
water the plant i have become
so someday i can be a tree
only your Word true poetry

rondel 287
2015

something of Me tell Me you see
then come and open up the door
a whole new universe explore
expanding your reality

do you know where you want to be
do you know what you're looking for
something of Me tell Me you see
then come and open up the door

you want to live a fantasy
do you not hear Me in you roar
why is it I you most ignore
why must you see to trust in Me
something of Me tell Me you see

kishion
2013

for she wants everything but Me
I just want her to be My bride
she has no clue of will what be
inside of the world she does hide

night and day for her have I cried
for she wants everything but Me
to My Word she never replied
now My accord to her cut free

in the past in My hands putty
I thought forever to abide
for she wants everything but Me
to Me I can no longer guide

with no belief what lacks inside
out of her life she has cut Me
she never will be satisfied
for she wants everything but Me

quatern 665
2020

until with Divinity swirled
we without wisdom ill fated
before us ever doom unfurled
our light within darkness faded

what we knew was overrated
until with Divinity swirled
it was our own minds we raided
upon our hearts the arrows hurled

before the truth within us thurled
throughout our own waste we waded
until with Divinity swirled
outside paradise we waited

but by our own flesh we aided
in our own hands we hold the world
which for ourselves we created
until with Divinity swirled

quatern 606
2020

you hold your world within your hand
before you red carpets unfurled
within your reach every demand
enthusiasts about you skirled

you chose the way your current birled
you hold your world within your hand
the waters toward or away purled
upon the island which you stand

it is yourself alone to strand
a truth for which your heart is thurled
you hold your world within your hand
to land upon at what it hurled

around your throat as fingers curled
the hour glass runs out of sand
til you know He who holds the world
you hold your world within your hand

rondel 351
2016

mostly sin comes from the tongue
evil inside of us stirs
wickedness of man endures
our nobility unsung

not to end when we were young
the nature of the flesh errs
mostly sin comes from the tongue
evil inside of us stirs

as if of the dead among
circling a wake of vultures
over us kindred cultures
from our own words spoken hung
mostly sin comes from the tongue

really
2010

it is the age that is evil
it is the flesh that is lazy
it is greed that begets envy
in anger cries out a mind full

of fantasy and fable
in gluttony begs the belly
it is the age that is evil
it is the flesh that is lazy

it is the eye that lust does pull
in anger cries out a mind free
a chance you never had really
it is pride that fills this vessel
it is the age that is evil

rondel 192
2014

in every sin pride is the broth
yet pride is taught to bring glory
lustful pride leads to adultery
while loathsome pride translates to wroth

gluttonous pride issues through sloth
greedy pride is love of money
in every sin pride is the broth
yet pride is taught to bring glory

false judgement and gossip is froth
covetous prides root is envy
selfish pride becomes vanity
conceit is cut from the same cloth
in every sin pride is the broth

the enemy
2019

to interrupt the plan of God
the woman the serpent beguiled
to prevent the birth of a child
pervert the lineage unflawed

the fruit of eve the world deceive
the garden the devil defiled
for the Son of God he reviled
a son for him did she conceive

out from the presence of the Lord
went and dwelt in the land of nod
there hidden from the face of God
he builded cities for his horde

angels kept not their first estate
their own habitation forsook
devils the daughters of men took
a new evil seed to create

men of renown wicked in way
begotten celestial strains
reserved in everlasting chains
til the judgement of that great day

quatern 486
2017

before the next coming of Christ
the son of perdition revealed
upon the most holy to feist
the fate of most by his mark sealed

the whole world to his demands yield
before the next coming of Christ
a flood of lies his mouth to wield
with flatteries his kingship heist

the harlot of this world enticed
his counterfeit religion build
before the next coming of Christ
his governmental system gild

in dark sentences is he skilled
brought up before him sacrificed
not my words to speak Spirit filled
before the next coming of Christ

ribbon
2011

when Jesus comes the flesh is dirt
but first the antichrist must come
playing Jesus do not play dumb
without truth with disaster flirt

the issue of it do not skirt
truth you cannot walk away from
when Jesus comes the flesh is dirt
but first the antichrist must come

to stay alive just stay alert
to his come hithers become numb
and with Jesus overcome or
find yourself in a world of hurt
when Jesus comes the flesh is dirt

rondel 597
2019

antichrist is coming first
wait for Jesus truth deduced
to eternal life induced
in the Word of God immersed

for the living waters thirst
from the fear of hades loosed
antichrist is coming first
wait for Jesus truth deduced

do not be as eve accursed
spiritually seduced
by the flood of lies reduced
rather by the bible versed
antichrist is coming first

rondel 326
2015

to know so long before he came
truly that he was coming first
within hypocrisy submersed
for coming in anothers name

without it but to die in shame
the truth for which so many thirst
to know so long before he came
truly that he was coming first

do not believe his royal claim
the role for so long he rehearsed
a destiny fated accursed
from within to be set aflame
to know so long before he came

rondel 264
2015

peacefully and prosperously
is how the antichrist premiers
with love conquering all frontiers
and the campaign slogan trust me

proclaiming come to set us free
when the one world in two shears
peacefully and prosperously
is how the antichrist premiers

within the Word and thus thusly
the whole earth his evil enspheres
an imposter the world reveres
before Jesus comes this must be
peacefully and prosperously

rancor
2013

that is the sixth seal trump and vial
the seventh has not yet arrived
the truth is here to be derived
the sixth again comes to beguile

facts overwhelmingly compile
something that could not be contrived
that is the sixth seal trump and vial
the seventh has not yet arrived

the devil cast down to defile
the time shortened or none survive
i believe in months about five
til the seventh remain nubile
that is the sixth seal trump and vial

rehearsed
2011

just the illusion of savior
the enemy is coming first
when the world is about to burst
when even elect may waver

and from all the kings gains favor
creating only souls accursed
just the illusion of savior
the enemy is coming first

watch closely at its behavior
like man its act is well rehearsed
fantasies and false dreams dispersed
listen close and hear it quaver
just the illusion of savior

rondel 251
2014

a prince he comes this world to rule
of darkness to venture false claim
to that which is not his by name
to hold the true Kings crowning jewel

a war of deception to fuel
pull all he can into the flame
a prince he comes this world to rule
of darkness to venture false claim

an ordained destiny to duel
in vanity the lust for fame
for every mans worship his aim
to be enthroned a jesting fool
a prince he comes this world to rule

quatern 130
2012

a beast in illusion arrayed
condemned and forsaken for pride
the one for whom eve was forbade
with greedy eyes glaring worldwide

when the earth and hell coincide
a beast in illusion arrayed
with predestined fate to collide
wandering a fruitless crusade

the enemy plans to invade
because no one will go untried
a beast in illusion arrayed
children of God in God confide

in circumstance one will abide
for evil judgement will be paid
time is short the demons untied
a beast in illusion arrayed

quatern 666
2020

to slay a third of men their soul
the sun turns as to sackcloth black
the blood red moon the fools extol
the stars upon the earth to smack

the great river of waters lack
to slay a third of men their soul
two million man army to sack
the kings of the east time to toll

the blowing smoke of mind control
deceptive black magic to stack
to slay a third of men their soul
out of the dragons mouth attack

the mountains and islands move back
the heavens roll up as a scroll
the great quake the whole earth to crack
to slay a third of men their soul

quatern 390
2016

the mystery unknown to man
the enemy appearing first
to beguile the world his plan
in mans desire being versed

within his lies the world submersed
the mystery unknown to man
while for water of life men thirst
his smoke across the world to fan

his stay for centuries to span
his claim to be god well rehearsed
the mystery unknown to man
as but truly spoken of erst

within his destruction accursed
he'll bring you along if he can
from within asunder to burst
the mystery unknown to man

rondel 666
2020

celestial darkness cross the land
when the light on the earth is dim
the fate of the fool yet then grim
a mark upon his head and hand

an entrance to all the world grand
the chance not to be deceived slim
celestial darkness cross the land
when the light on the earth is dim

the great dragon soon cast out and
his angels too cast out with him
within the sea to rage and swim
but for the wise to understand
celestial darkness cross the land

quatern 315
2015

the enemy will be about
deception in a heap to mound
from a beguiling mouth to spout
a twisting of the truth unwound

with miracles man to astound
the enemy will be about
prosperity and peace then found
for those to him will be devout

to be every mans god his flout
of kings of this world to be crowned
the enemy will be about
til feet of Jesus touch the ground

the sixth scroll will soon be unbound
the sixth vial will be poured out
the sixth trumpet will shortly sound
the enemy will be about

quatern 633
2020

allow not the enemy in
he comes to destroy and deceive
his prey lives underneath the skin
of his being be not naive

his artifice worldwide to weave
allow not the enemy in
the victory yours to achieve
if from the whirl of the world spin

wave and wield Yeshua and win
salvation from His sheath relieve
allow not the enemy in
pray for protection and believe

the strength of the Spirit retrieve
from fore the flesh age did begin
upon the promise of God cleave
allow not the enemy in

quatern 445
2017

the man with the magical tongue
dangling every bedazzling word
captivating the old and young
oblivious of what occurred

a caldron of enchantment stirred
the man with the magical tongue
of all charming fantasies heard
best balladesque mystery sung

adrift in transport tales among
intent intentionally blurred
the man with the magical tongue
muffled mesmerism murmured

goading goats false sentiment spurred
guiding through gardens of but dung
only to the elect absurd
the man with the magical tongue

rondel 639
2020

when the moon conceals the light of the sun
blood red it to turn for he is with man
the flesh age sojourn according to plan
the black veil reveals the end has begun

the waters will churn horizons to pan
from darkness one feels unable to run
when the moon conceals the light of the sun
blood red it to turn for he is with man

the world blinded kneels before the wrong one
deception to burn across the globe fan
with flatteries earn all the kings he can
the enemy steals souls til it is done
when the moon conceals the light of the sun

rondel 520
2018

unto the lowest hell beware
on fire the mountains foundation
burnt with a hunger uncommon
devoured with burning heat where

upon them teeth of beast do tear
and serpent of the dust poison
unto the lowest hell beware
on fire the mountains foundation

with bitter destruction to bear
the sword without terror within
shall destroy young man and virgin
the suckling and man of grey hair
unto the lowest hell beware

ravenous
2013

beware the fowl of the air
beware the beast of the field
brandishing weapons concealed
tread carefully through their lair

demons that do not fight fair
those whose fate already sealed
beware the fowl of the air
beware the beast of the field

discover a truth to bear
the sword of the Lord to wield
with His righteousness your shield
do not intertwine with tare
beware the fowl of the air

rondel 568
2019

there is no end of the east
forever proceeds the west
the north and south at poles rest
where their direction deceased

velocity has increased
east and west ever abreast
there is no end of the east
forever proceeds the west

even so amidst the least
with abundant bounty blessed
salvation to end the quest
as a never ending feast
there is no end of the east

the end
2019

sewing veils to put over eyes
from out of their own hearts am I
against daughters who prophesy
lie to whom they love hearing lies

to save the souls which should not live
for gain slay souls which should not die
they hunt the souls to make them fly
and hide deliverance I give

the enemy sows tares among
the wheat and then he goes his way
they grow together til the day
the harvest song is to be sung

gathered together the tares are
first and bound in bundles to burn
then the wheat are gathered in turn
into the barn of God afar

rondel 499
2017

when death and time do not exist
the age to come an age sublime
for all this clockworks final chime
into eternity to twist

rise above primordial mist
the vine of flesh no more to climb
when death and time do not exist
the age to come an age sublime

unless your chance to go is missed
going to be there i know i'm
the death of death and death of time
i wonder if you get the gist
when death and time do not exist

quatern 208
2014

already lost a third of time
obviously another sign
that on this age the bell will chime
soon will come the glorious shine

of this event am i found fine
already lost a third of time
a third of moonlight and sunshine
to alter assumed paradigm

to shorten impossible climb
to hasten the coming deadline
already lost a third of time
what but could be of the divine

when all that will at last align
and bring about an age sublime
the earth has shifted by design
already lost a third of time

rondel 655
2020

the Lords day is but once
yet everyday the Lords
bestowing just rewards
every conscience confronts

a sifting of all stunts
refining of all swords
the Lords day is but once
yet everyday the Lords

the end of all their hunts
upon the evil horde
for all they are awards
upon whom all affronts
the Lords day is but once

quatern 396
2016

until the second advent, from
tribulation preservation
the axis of the earths brought plumb
bringing complete restoration

under divine conservation
until the second advent, from
the enemy liberation
unafraid of the battle drum

spotless for this spirit to come
in the soon regeneration
until the second advent, from
transgression emancipation

the meaning of life, salvation
misfortunate for a great some
a depraved age extrication
until the second advent from

quatern 204
2014

Your wonders the world will witness
hail of a hundred pounds will fall
only upon Your elect miss
the fools still blind as You enthrall

the sun and moon and stars withdrawal
Your wonders the world will witness
night and day no longer crawl
within my heart to believe this

the opening of the abyss
sea creatures dying great and small
Your wonders the world will witness
the greatest mountains burning tall

the earth quakes with a caterwaul
for whom they know the coming bliss
Your advent in every eyeball
Your wonders the world will witness

rondel 431
2017

fear He whose voice shall shake the earth
the signs now seen sound the alarm
do not trust in this ages charm
for no future is in the firth

all waters to be total dearth
while men for fading trinkets smarm
fear He whose voice shall shake the earth
the signs now seen sound the alarm

all the heavens Yeshuas girth
my trust shall be upon His arm
in wrath remembers mercies worth
fear not what can cause but flesh harm
fear He whose voice shall shake the earth

kilter
2013

right the earth with perfect balance
the ground so move the waters churn
to purify rudiments rinse
from all the evil which You spurn

for in this age we but sojourn
right the world with perfect balance
from just and unjust to discern
from end to the beginning since

make the heavens above to wince
the whole face of the world to burn
right the earth with perfect balance
it is for this the elect yearn

bestow to each for that they earn
bind and imprison this worlds prince
upon the day of Your return
right the world with perfect balance

rondel 271
2015

to shed this flesh as winter fur
and feel the earth become upright
on its axis in endless light
sights to forever enamor

spiting darkness to share the cure
upon the cold will come a blight
to shed this flesh as winter fur
and feel the earth become upright

for once again to become pure
elements no more of the night
a glory comes to end the plight
upon the last trump to occur
to shed this flesh as winter fur

rondel 401
2016

when the four winds come
this age is no more
the end of this chore
from the flesh freedom

peace and joy for some
for others a war
when the four winds come
this age is no more

to push all back plumb
a broad cup to pour
the last shofars roar
Gods righteous lips from
when the four winds come

rondel 455
2017

the world will not end
but simply the age
the turn of a page
a message to send

the One to defend
to witness His rage
the world will not end
but simply the age

this spirit to mend
release from this cage
upon the grand stage
from the flesh to rend
the world will not end

rondel 624
2020

the war is but for a moment
the victory is forever
pull upon this age the lever
and for it never to lament

so far beyond a lifetime spent
for than themselves those more clever
the war is but for a moment
the victory is forever

the battle of flesh dissever
no more behind the rampart pent
the boundary between us rent
for paradise to endeavor
the victory is forever

rondel 644
2020

when this sinful age full
a time no other braved
evil of the unsaved
most unfathomable

nature then unstable
the earth from within caved
when this sinful age full
a time no other braved

upon minds His label
His Word on hearts engraved
the way to heaven paved
within paradise pull
when this sinful age full

rondel 590
2019

enter into eternal bliss
paradise for you were aching
tumult before ever breaking
abandoned in obscure abyss

all secluded outcast amiss
slumber the unrest forsaking
enter into eternal bliss
paradise for you were aching

deserted in your oasis
a wilderness of own making
on the verge of awakening
thundering disquiets last hiss
enter into eternal bliss

quatern 569
2019

unto the one true God a wife
a new divine age to begin
the wonder all about us rife
this ages clockwork wearing thin

the wedding day is closing in
unto the one true God a wife
open the sky and show me heaven
cut through the dark cloud as a knife

carry me through the burning strife
around heavenly orbit spin
unto the one true God a wife
a divine heavenly union

the war foretold which we will win
this imperfection put on life
another paid the price of sin
unto the one true God a wife

rondel 620
2020

caught up in the breath of life
within a cloud of angel
when sin has come to the full
no more the feeling of strife

the finish of gun and knife
to a new age God to pull
caught up in the breath of life
within a cloud of angel

made herself ready His wife
theories of men unravel
to jerusalem travel
with every believer rife
caught up in the breath of life

rondel 208
2014

the diviners have seen a lie
in vanity have told false dreams
perversion of truth with pride teams
for the innocent to defy

in sorcery to testify
in devising enchanted schemes
the diviners have seen a lie
in vanity have told false dreams

peer from behind an evil eye
in illusion to charm it seems
instructing inaccurate themes
the way to bliss to falsify
the diviners have seen a lie

rondel 523
2018

in search of verity to find
and yet never to fare thee well
to solid ground from clouds rappel
the bounds of fantasy unbind

the traditions of men unwind
the lies throughout the skies to quell
in search of stronger truth to find
and yet never to fare thee well

the noises in the dark remind
beyond the walls the rodents dwell
and every creeping thing as well
through cracks to leave their world behind
in search of better fare to find

quatern 612
2020

a dream ushering in nightmare
but an illusion of escape
fantasize to vanish in air
behind a black magicians cape

the perfect intention misshape
a dream ushering in nightmare
the surface of salvation scrape
all which is beneath to forbear

of all the false teachers beware
for filthy lucre children jape
a dream ushering in nightmare
untruth over saving hands drape

the door for the devil agape
unprepared for his time to fare
all of the naive virgins rape
a dream ushering in nightmare

quatern 491
2017

there is but one way home from here
over mountain and canyon gash
through wilderness and forest fear
frigid tundra and desert clash

a vast ocean within to splash
there is but one way home from here
as gerridae midst tidal crash
across the sea so cavalier

beyond the clouds and atmosphere
surpass the stars sparkle and flash
there is but one way home from here
about the universe to dash

with patience without being brash
in meadow full of peace appear
or within the lake of fire thrash
there is but one way home from here

rondel 489
2017

upon a virgin soil in route
a renaissance no more to stay
the sun standing before at bay
with an eerie moonglow in bout

naked over a shroud of doubt
a casting off of cloaks of clay
upon a virgin soil in route
a renaissance no more to stay

about this passage shadows stout
a darkened past eclipsed by a
future wandered throughout the day
the black before me blotted out
upon a virgin soil in route

rondel 245
2014

more much than ancient men to dream
deem which is to be evermore
screaming in chosen minds to bore
roaring the words of the Supreme

before all which man does esteem
streams of living waters ashore
more much than ancient men to dream
deem which is to be evermore

a new age is coming to seem
as if amidst nuclear war
melting the flesh to the ground pour
releasing our true selves to gleam
much more than ancient men to dream

rondel 654
2020

the fools believe this age
will go on forever
but for greed endeavor
they ever as wars wage

no blame for their rampage
they think themselves clever
the fools believe this age
will go on forever

with Yeshua engage
reality sever
eternity lever
endless existence stage
the fools believe this age

rejoice
2011

i cannot wait to laugh with You
and warm in Your glorious light
come in out of this cold dark night
to see the earth become anew

to know the truth men misconstrue
to end the innocent mans plight
i cannot wait to laugh with You
and warm in Your glorious light

find out what is Your point of view
get lost in the words which You might
offer ot me of what is right
and everything You say is true
i cannot wait to laugh with You

reward
2011

with You i long to live in bliss
and for that only You i serve
all that is good You will preserve
i thank You for Your forgiveness

Your love and gifts and righteousness
that to which i do not deserve
with You i long to live in bliss
and for that only You i serve

thank You for the darkness i miss
and all the beauty i observe
Your strength it is which gives me nerve
to get to You through all of this
with You i long to live in bliss

renegade
2011

mighty with God given wisdom
unfathomable for your mind
and so in everything behind
except the things i would run from

in the distance i hear the drum
of the war to which you are blind
mighty with God given wisdom
unfathomable for your mind

a destiny only for some
He is waiting for you to find
the way to Him which He designed
and to everlasting life come
mighty with God given wisdom

rondel 180
2014

it is not death for which i fear
it is life without Jesus, i
do not understand others why
try to deny that which is clear

He spoke His Word into my ear
He revealed Himself to my eye
it is not death for which i fear
it is life without Jesus, i
beyond the flesh to heaven peer
and so leave the world behind, my
spirit alive never to die
never again to shed a tear
it is not death for which i fear

rondel 613
2020

i see the end
last opened seal
darkness they feel
the heavens bend

the earth to rend
around to reel
i see the end
last opened seal

truth comprehend
every man kneel
the earth to heal
with heaven blend
i see the end